NATIONAL GEOGRAPHIC

# Ladders

# THE MAYA

## Pre-Columbian Americans

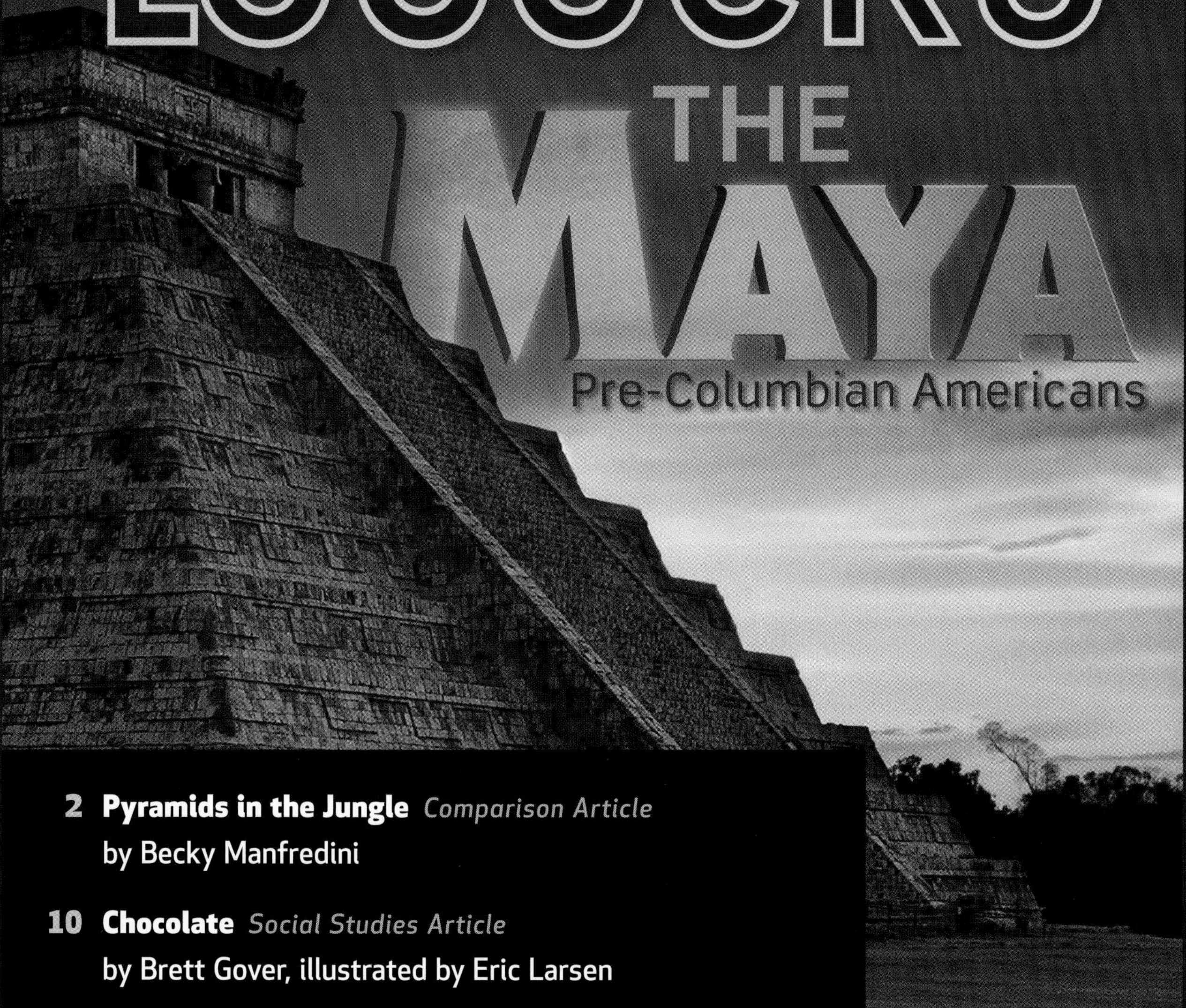

GENRE Comparison Article

**Read to find out** how pyramids of the Maya compare to those of ancient Egypt.

# PYRAMIDS IN THE JUNGLE

*by Becky Manfredini*

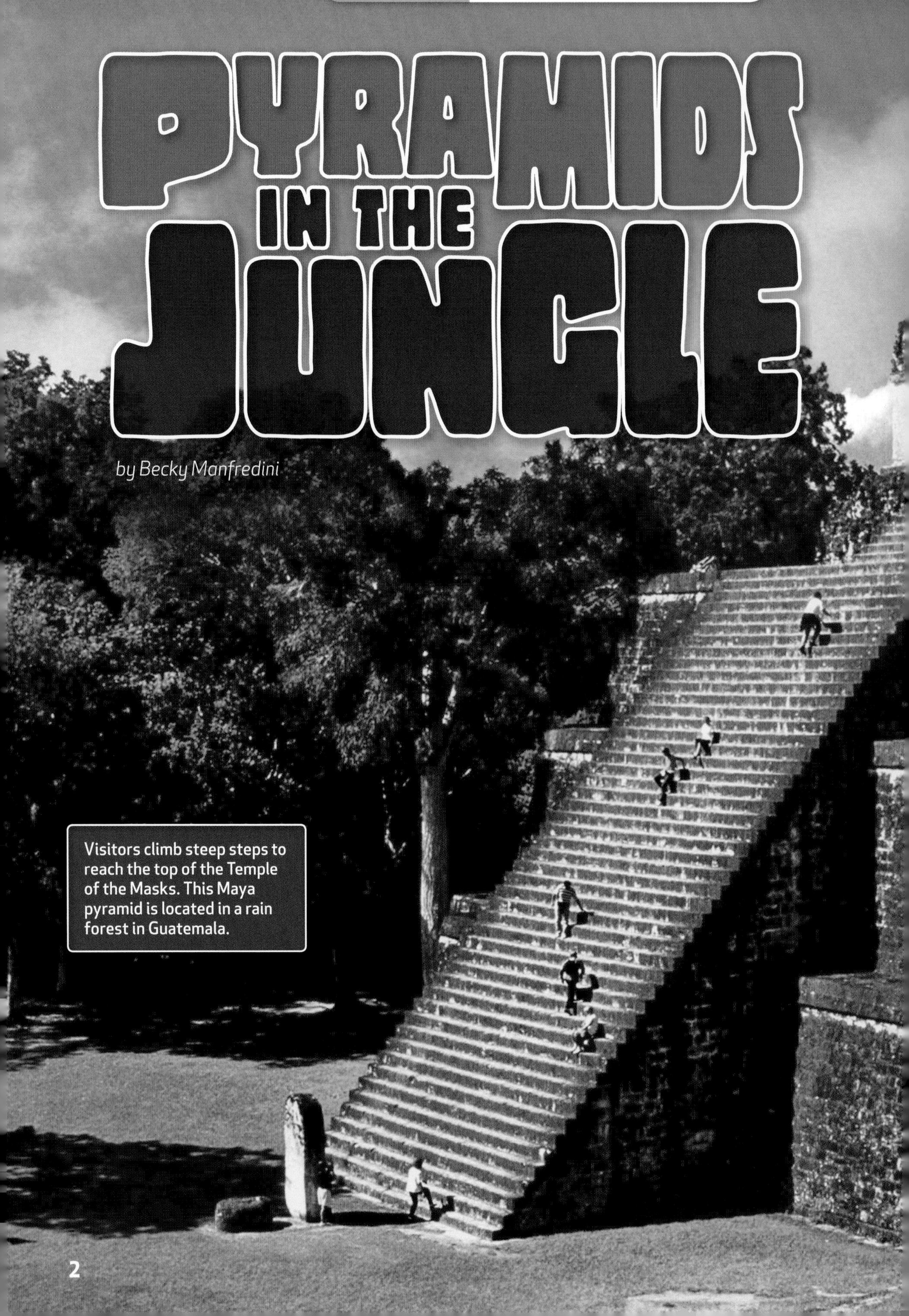

Visitors climb steep steps to reach the top of the Temple of the Masks. This Maya pyramid is located in a rain forest in Guatemala.

When you think of pyramids, ancient Egypt's great pyramids probably come to mind first. But another group of people called the Maya built pyramids, too. The Maya lived across the Atlantic Ocean in **Mesoamerica**. Mesoamerica, which means "middle America," was a cultural region that included parts of present-day Mexico and Central America.

The Maya pyramids were just as amazing as the ones built by the ancient Egyptians, but the Maya built them for different reasons. Ancient Egyptian pharaohs (FAIR-ohz), or leaders, built their pyramids as **tombs**. After they died, the pharaohs were buried deep inside the pyramids, surrounded by many treasures. The pyramids were then closed off to protect the pharaohs' bodies and treasures.

The Maya also used some pyramids as tombs, but more often, these magnificent structures were places for the Maya to worship and celebrate. Maya pyramids were built in the centers of cities. They were built very tall so people could see what was happening on them.

The ancient Egyptians stopped building pyramids around 2100 B.C. People began building pyramids in Mesoamerica 1,100 years later. It's a mystery how these two civilizations built such similar structures in different times and places.

# EGYPTIAN PYRAMIDS

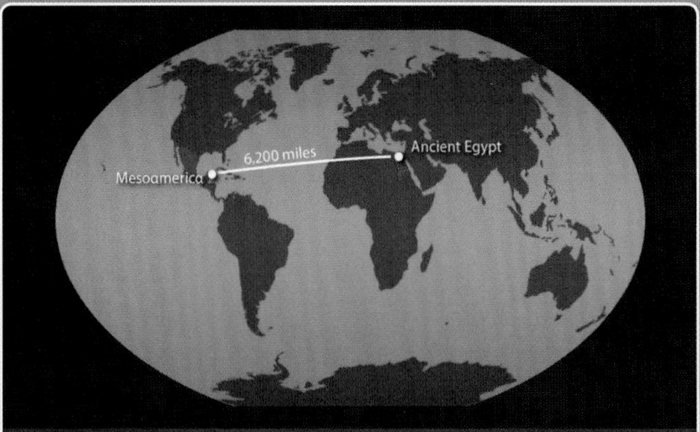


About 6,200 miles separate the pyramids of ancient Egypt from the pyramids of Mesoamerica.

The ancient Egyptians built the pyramids of Giza to last for a long time. In fact, the three gigantic pyramids in Giza, Egypt, have proudly guarded their spots in the desert for more than 4,500 years. Built as secure tombs for three ancient pharaohs, they have many interesting features.

Most ancient Egyptian pyramids were built one layer of stone at a time. As many as 100,000 workers dug up and cut each stone to be roughly the same size and shape. They used ropes and wooden sleds to drag the two-ton stones up a ramp. It took about 20 years to build the largest of the pyramids!

The ancient Egyptians located their pyramids away from cities. They built the Giza pyramids outside the ancient city of Memphis, Egypt.

# Maya Pyramids

Today, many Maya pyramids are hidden in jungles far away from modern cities. But at the time they were constructed, they were the heart of Maya cities. The Maya often painted the pyramids bright colors and added carvings and statues to set them apart from other buildings. Some had staircases so tall they seemed to touch the sky. Examples of decorated pyramids can be found in a Maya city named Palenque (pah-LEHN-kay).

Rising from the ground in layered steps, the pyramids of Palenque have watched over eastern Mexico since A.D. 600. To build them, workers gathered stones from the thick jungle surrounding the city. They piled the differently sized stones on top of each other to build the pyramids' walls.

Over the centuries, the bright red and blue paint has worn off of the Maya pyramids of Palenque. Archaeologists believe the Maya painted the Temple of Inscriptions, shown below, a deep red.

# MONUMENTS OF THE MAYA

The ancient Egyptian pyramids look very similar, but the Maya pyramids are all different shapes and sizes. Made to honor gods and kings, some pyramids still stand as examples of the Maya's excellent building skills. Let's take a closer look at three different pyramids from three different Maya cities in Mesoamerica: El Tigre (TEE-gray) in the city of El Mirador, the Temple of the Great Jaguar in the city of Tikal (tee-KAHL), and El Castillo (kah-STEE-yoh) in the city of Tulum (too-LOOM).

**EL TIGRE** Between 600 B.C. and A.D. 150, a Maya city called El Mirador thrived in the dense rain forest of present-day Guatemala. One of the largest buildings in the city, standing 180 feet tall, was the pyramid called El Tigre—The Tiger. A broad platform and three small temples sat on top of El Tigre. Huge humanlike and catlike masks adorned these small temples. Maya kings performed ceremonies in different areas of the platform on the pyramid. The outer walls glimmered bright red under the hot sun, while elaborate pictures decorated the walls inside.

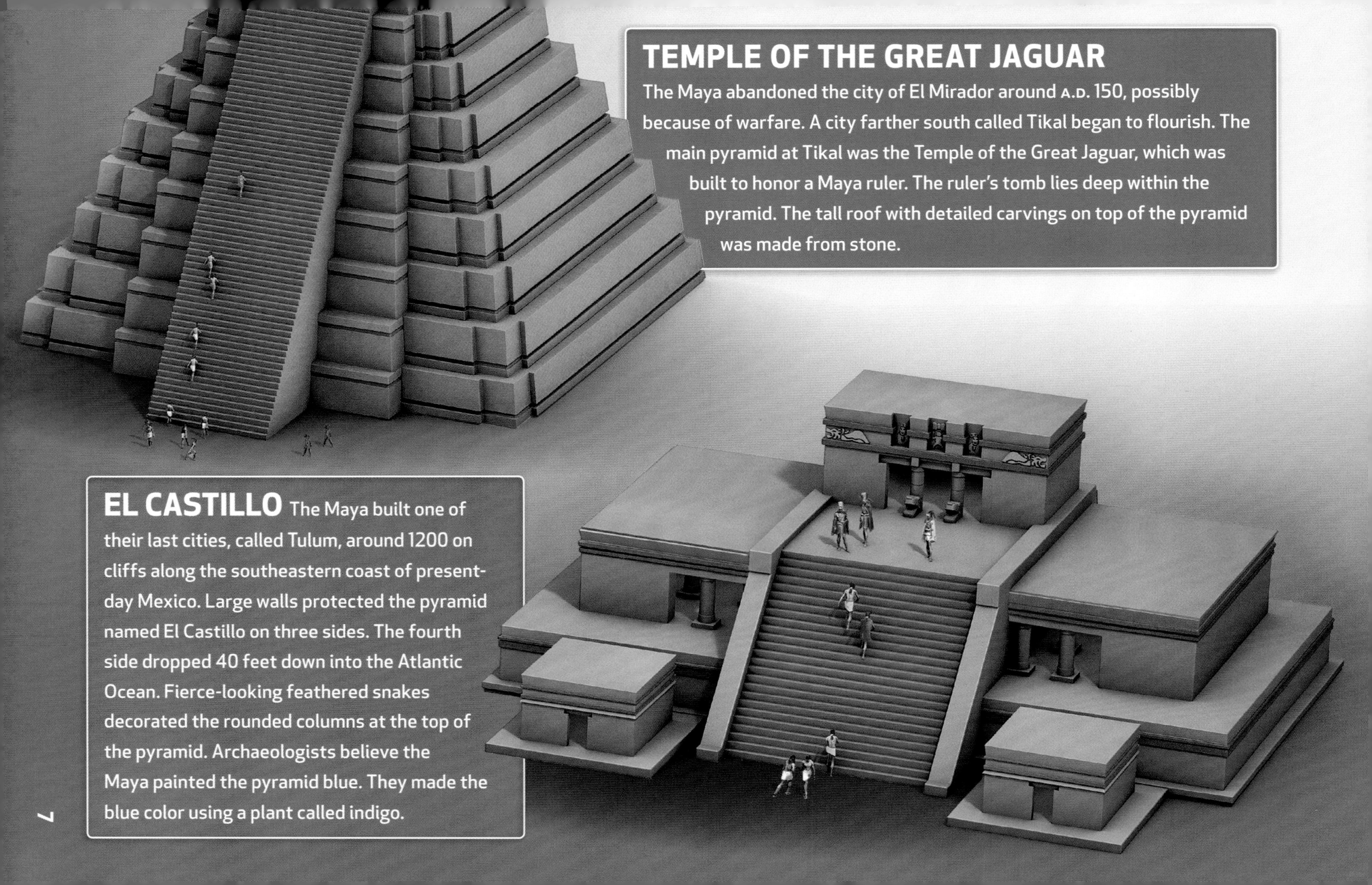

## TEMPLE OF THE GREAT JAGUAR

The Maya abandoned the city of El Mirador around A.D. 150, possibly because of warfare. A city farther south called Tikal began to flourish. The main pyramid at Tikal was the Temple of the Great Jaguar, which was built to honor a Maya ruler. The ruler's tomb lies deep within the pyramid. The tall roof with detailed carvings on top of the pyramid was made from stone.

**EL CASTILLO** The Maya built one of their last cities, called Tulum, around 1200 on cliffs along the southeastern coast of present-day Mexico. Large walls protected the pyramid named El Castillo on three sides. The fourth side dropped 40 feet down into the Atlantic Ocean. Fierce-looking feathered snakes decorated the rounded columns at the top of the pyramid. Archaeologists believe the Maya painted the pyramid blue. They made the blue color using a plant called indigo.

# Swallowed by the Jungle

Unlike the pyramids of ancient Egypt that rise above the sandy desert, the Maya pyramids hide in the lush greenery of the jungle. Plentiful sunlight and heavy rains cause plants to grow very quickly in the surrounding rain forest. Some of the pyramids were discovered only by accident when travelers stumbled across them in the jungle.

A Spanish priest discovered the Temple of the Great Jaguar in 1695 when he got lost in the rain forest. He passed through the ruins of the city of Tikal and became the first European to see its astonishing buildings. The jungle hid other Maya structures, too. The pyramids and other buildings in the city of El Mirador looked like steep hills until an engineer unearthed part of a building in 1885.

More recently, still more pyramids were discovered using advanced technology. The San Bartolo pyramid is located northeast of the ruins of Tikal. Many Maya lived in the area from about 600 B.C. to A.D. 900. Archaeologists used **GPS** mapping to locate the ruins in 2011. GPS (Global Positioning System) is a satellite system that helps locate places and shows them on **3D**, or three dimensional, maps. GPS and 3D mapping revealed the San Bartolo ruins swallowed by the jungle.

This illustration of the San Bartolo pyramid was made using GPS and 3D mapping. It shows what the pyramid may have looked like hundreds of years ago.

The Maya built a room decorated with **murals**, or pictures painted on walls, beneath the San Bartolo pyramid.

**Check In** How did the pyramids in Maya cities differ from one another?

GENRE Social Studies Article **Read to find out** where chocolate comes from and how it is made.

# Choco

*by Brett Gover illustrated by Eric Larsen*

Where does chocolate come from? You might be surprised to learn that chocolate actually grows on a tree. But this amazing tree doesn't sprout chocolate bars. Let's find out what it really does.

Chocolate comes from the seeds of the **cacao** (kuh-KOW) tree. This tree once grew only in the rain forests of Central and South America. But in recent centuries, chocolate lovers have planted it in other tropical regions of the world.

Reaching only 20 to 40 feet in the air, the cacao tree is smaller than many other trees in the rain forest. The cacao tree would grow taller if it weren't for the rain forest's **canopy**. The canopy is made up of the branches and leaves of the tallest trees. The shade of the canopy blocks sunlight from the shorter plants, and without that added sunlight, a cacao tree cannot grow any taller.

If you look at a blooming cacao tree, you'll see bright flowers of white, pink, and red. The flowers grow out of the trunk and older branches. After four months, the flowers grow into football-shaped pods that are a little longer than a man's hand. The pods ripen in about five months. Each one produces 20 to 60 seeds, called cacao beans.

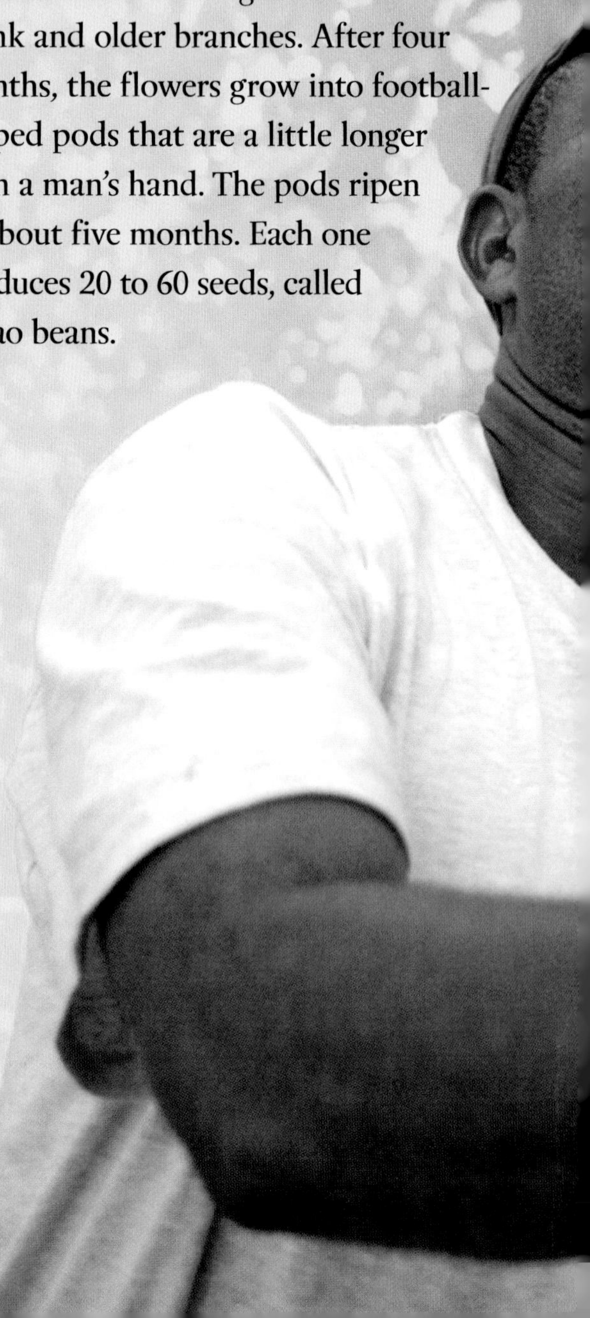

A man plucks a cacao pod from a tree in the Dominican Republic, a country located in the Caribbean.

# late

# From Cacao Bean to Candy Bar

The idea of chocolate bars growing on trees is silly, of course. But how do the seeds of the cacao tree become the rich, smooth chocolate we all love?

**1.** Cacao farmers use a knife or stick to knock the ripe pods from the cacao tree. The brightly colored pods soon turn brown.

**4.** Next, the beans are roasted in an oven to give them a richer flavor and a deeper color. Then workers remove the shells. What's left is called the nib.

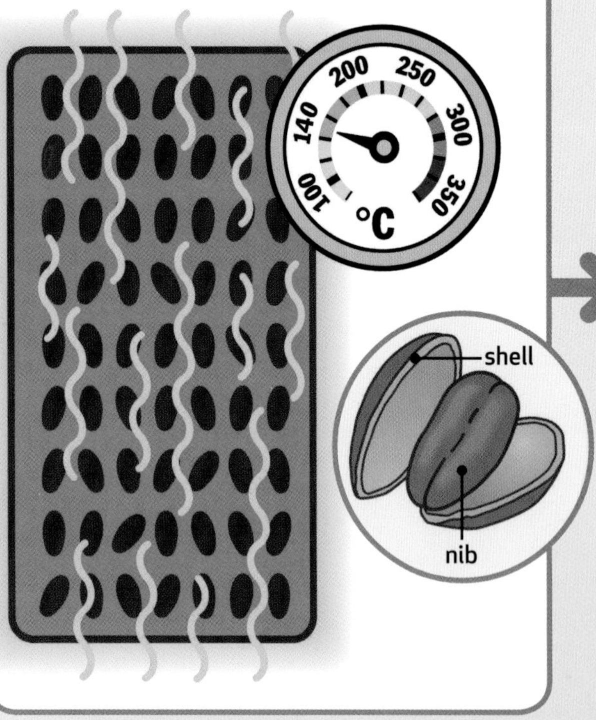


**5.** Workers grind the nibs and use heat and pressure to squeeze two liquids out of them. One is a dark brown liquid called chocolate liquor. The other is a clear liquid called cocoa butter. Cocoa butter does not have a taste or smell, but it makes the chocolate feel smooth when it's eaten.

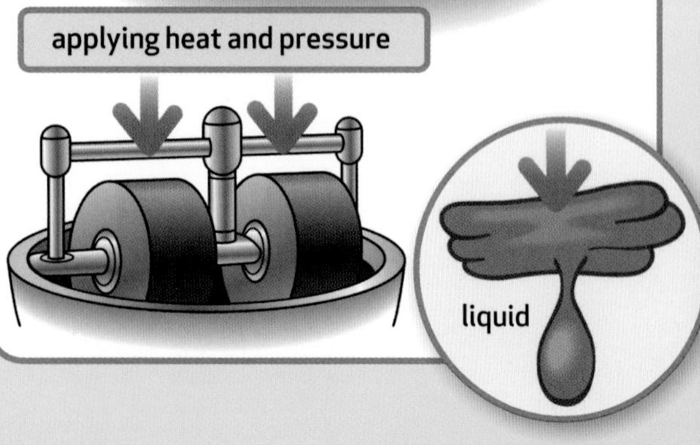

**2.** Next, the farmers split open the pods and remove the cacao beans. They heap the beans together, cover them with leaves, and allow them to **ferment**, or rot, for a few days. That breaks down the beans.

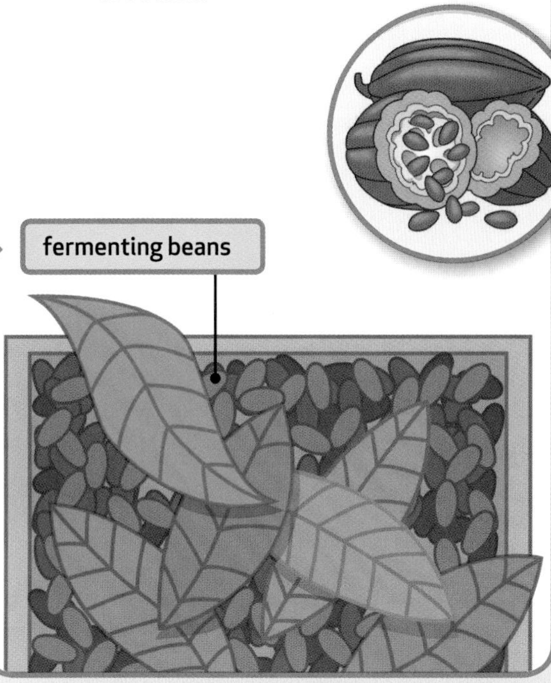


**3.** Then the farmers dry the fermented beans in the sun or in an oven. They clean them to get rid of twigs and stones.

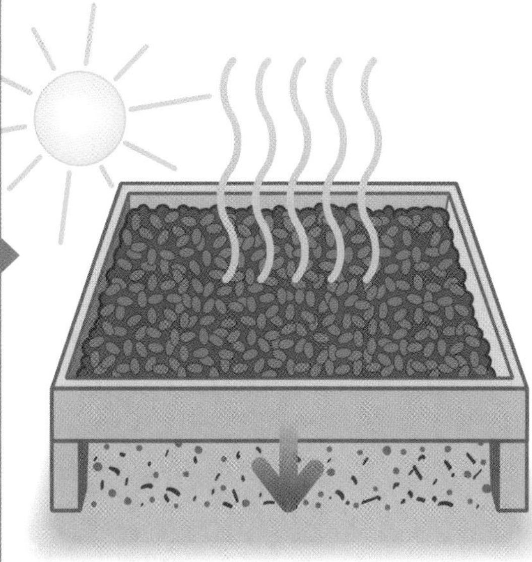

**6.** To make milk chocolate, workers add cocoa butter, sugar, and milk to the chocolate liquor. They blend the liquor and the cocoa butter together. They press and knead the mixture between two rollers to give it a smooth texture.

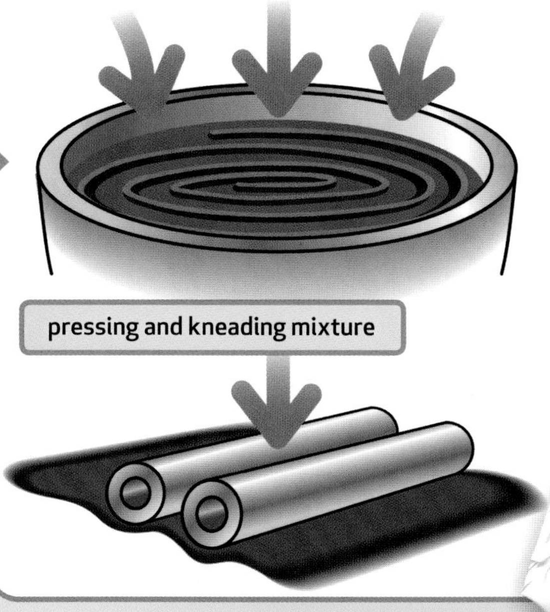


**7.** Next, workers heat and stir the mixture continuously for 12 hours or longer and then pour it into molds shaped like candy bars. After the bars have cooled and become solid, workers put wrappers around them, place them in boxes, and send them off to the stores where they will be sold.

# A Gift from the Gods

The Maya certainly thought chocolate was delicious, but they also considered it a gift from the gods. They even worshipped a god of the cacao tree and its pods. This civilization valued chocolate so highly that the cacao bean became a **currency**, or a form of money. People used cacao beans to buy goods and services.

Cacao trees growing wild in the rain forest did not supply enough cacao beans to meet the Maya's needs. So they cleared large areas of forest and planted groves of the trees. Like chocolate makers today, they dried and roasted the cacao beans and then ground the nibs. They often combined the chocolate liquor with cornmeal and flavorings such as chile peppers, vanilla, honey, and spices. The recipe made a bitter, zesty drink. The thick, bubbly foam that formed when this drink was poured was considered the tastiest part. The Maya served the drink in special pitchers during religious ceremonies.

This serving pitcher was crafted in the shape of the Maya god of cacao.

This Maya mural shows people preparing and drinking chocolate. The Maya believed the drink cured many illnesses and they weren't wrong. Today, scientists are discovering more and more healthy benefits to eating chocolate.

When Spanish explorers arrived in Mesoamerica in the 1500s, they drank chocolate for the first time. They liked it so much they brought it back to Spain. By the 1600s, the desire for chocolate had spread to other parts of Europe.

Soon, people throughout Europe began creating their own tasty foods and drinks from the cacao bean. For example, the Spanish replaced the spices that the Maya added to their chocolate with sugar. In the 1800s, Europeans added milk to their chocolate. The sweet, milky drink that resulted was probably very similar to the hot chocolate people enjoy today.

We consume chocolate in many different ways, such as in candy bars and ice cream. Unsweetened chocolate is used to flavor meat dishes and is also an important ingredient in some of the *mole* (MOH-lay) sauces popular in Mexican cooking. Chocolate might not be sacred to people today, but our world would be a lot less delicious without it!

**Check In** What are the steps involved in making chocolate?

**GENRE** Historical Tour

**Read to find out** about a historical Maya site.

# A TOUR OF Chiché

This aerial view shows the ruins of Chichén Itzá, a city that tens of thousands of people once called home.

*by Elizabeth Massie*

Welcome to Chichén Itzá (chee-CHEN eet-ZAH)! Today we'll be touring the ruins of this great city. Between A.D. 750 and 1200, Chichén Itzá was the most powerful Maya city of them all. It was the New York City of its time—a dazzling, bustling center filled with people and businesses of all kinds. Hundreds of years later, visitors remain fascinated with the city and its history.

Chichén Itzá is located on Mexico's Yucatán (yoo-kuh-TAN) Peninsula. A **peninsula** is a landform that is surrounded on three sides by water. The Yucatán Peninsula extends into the Gulf of Mexico. The Maya built Chichén Itzá on the Yucatán Peninsula in the 600s, where it served as a center of culture, trade, government, and religion. The city remained powerful until the late 1500s, when the Maya abandoned it. It sat undisturbed by humans and protected by the jungle that surrounds it for nearly 300 years.

In the mid-1800s, archaeologists began to explore and **excavate**, or dig out, this sacred site. Since then, they have taken great care to preserve the ruins that remain. Archaeologists excavate sites like Chichén Itzá so people who live now can learn about people who lived in the past. Today, Chichén Itzá is a popular attraction that draws thousands of tourists from around the world.

# The Kukulkán Pyramid

The Kukulkán (kuh-kool-KAHN) Pyramid is one of the most impressive structures in Chichén Itzá. This pyramid sits in the Great **Plaza**, or central court, of the city, honoring the feathered serpent god, Quetzalcóatl (KWET-sul-kuh-WAH-tul).

The Kukulkán Pyramid towers 79 feet above the jungle floor. Four sets of 91 steps on each of the pyramid's sides lead to the top. If you add up all the steps, you get 364. If you then include the top platform, the total number is 365, which represents the days of a yearly calendar.

A huge stone sculpture of Quetzalcóatl's head sits at the base of the pyramid. Twice a year, at the beginning of spring and fall, a curious thing happens. As the

A sculpture called a *chacmool* guards the Kukulkán Pyramid at Chichén Itzá. Found throughout Central America, many chacmools hold cups on their bellies. Archaeologists believe the Maya left gifts to their gods in the cups.

sun sets, a shadow slowly crawls down the stairs of the pyramid. The shadow is shaped like the body of a serpent. At the bottom, the shadow body connects to the sculpture of the serpent's head. It's an impressive sight. The Maya must have known a lot about shadows, architecture, and the seasons in order to create this amazing show.

This carved image shows Quetzalcóatl, the feathered serpent god of the Maya.

# El Caracol

One thing is for sure—the Maya were great **astronomers**, or scientists who study the sun, stars, and planets. In fact, just like astronomers today, they dedicated entire buildings to the study of the sky.

Built between A.D. 600 and 850, El Caracol (el kah-rah-KOL) was an observatory, a place where Maya astronomers studied the sun, stars, and planets. Like many modern observatories, it is tall, round, and constructed on a square platform. The height of the building rose above the trees of the jungle and the building's rounded top allowed early astronomers to see the sky from every possible angle.

El Caracol has three tiny windows in its highest tower. These windows allowed Maya astronomers to observe important things in the sky, such as the exact spot of the sunset on the equinoxes, which are the two days of the year when there is the same number of hours of daylight and darkness.

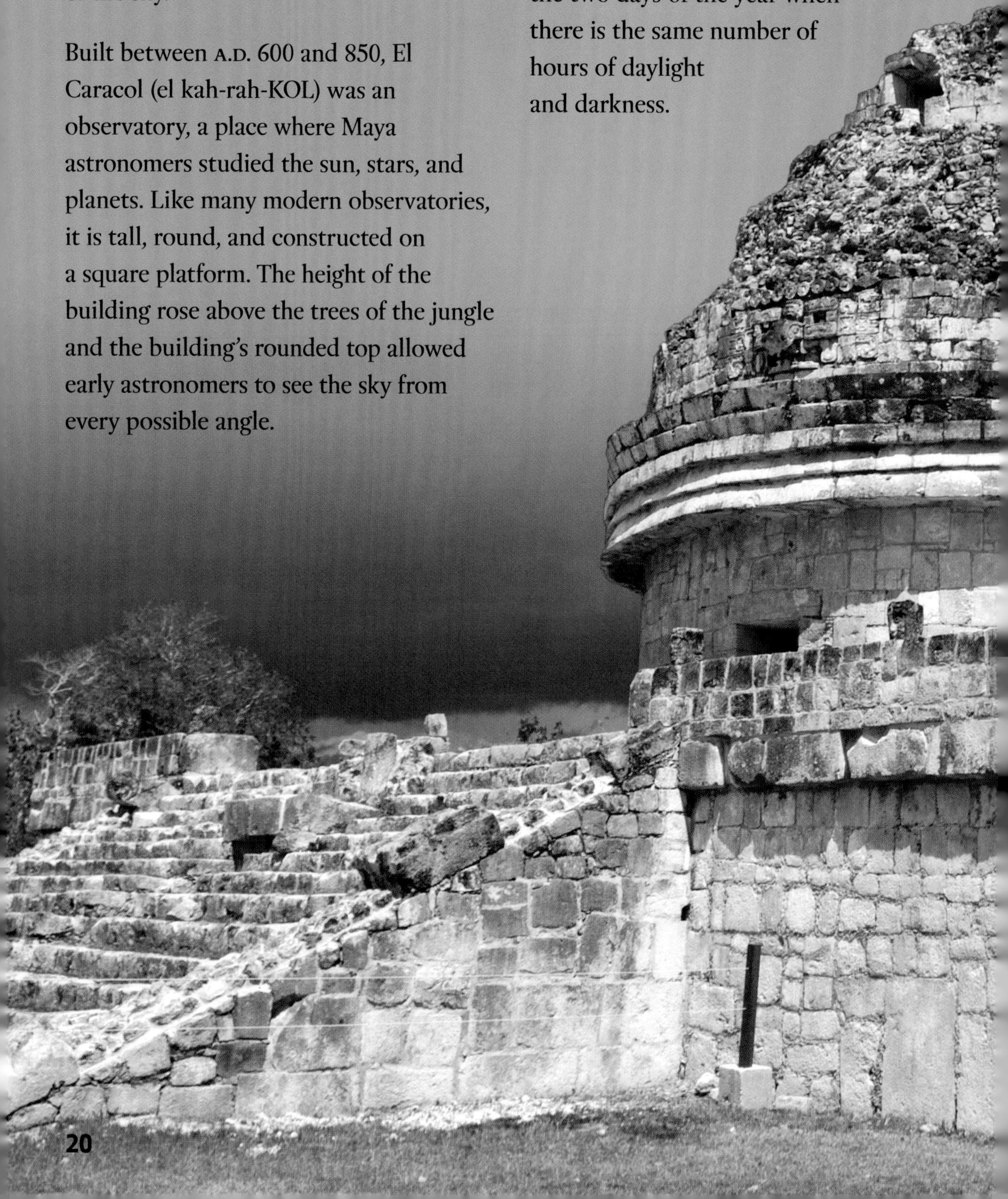

By observing the sky from El Caracol, the Maya correctly figured out Earth's solar year, or how long it takes Earth to revolve once around the sun. The Maya also predicted solar eclipses. On Earth, a solar eclipse is when the moon passes in front of the sun, blocking the sun's light for a short time. Even today, astronomers are amazed by the Maya's knowledge of the movements in the skies.

The McDonald Observatory in Fort Davis, Texas, resembles El Caracol.

El Caracol means "the snail." Inside El Caracol is a winding staircase. The stairs look like the spiral inside a snail's shell.

# The Great Ball Court

Ball games are popular around the world. People of all ages enjoy playing basketball, baseball, soccer, and football. The Maya played an especially exciting—and for some, dangerous—ball game.

The Great Ball Court at Chichén Itzá is the largest remaining Mesoamerican ball court. It is made of stone and shaped like a long rectangle with small nooks at each corner. The sloping walls of the court stretch 554 feet long and 231 feet wide, which is larger than a football field.

^ This sculpture of a Maya ball player shows the protective clothing he wore during a game.

We don't know what the exact rules of this Maya ball game were, but we have an idea based on drawings the Maya left behind and ball games people in the region play today. The game may have been played like soccer. The ball was made of sap from nearby rubber trees and weighed as much as 20 pounds. Players were not allowed to touch the ball with their hands.

The court had large hoops sticking out on either long side of the rectangle. The goal of the game was to kick the ball through the hoops, high on the walls.

Competition in today's ball games can be intense, but lives were at stake during these early Maya ball games. The losers of the game were often killed, but the winners were respected as heroes.

A stone hoop in the Great Ball Court is set about 20 feet above the ground. The hoop's height made it challenging to score a point.

**Check In** Explain some of the knowledge the Maya had about astronomy.

**GENRE** **Science Article** **Read to find out** about underwater archaeology.

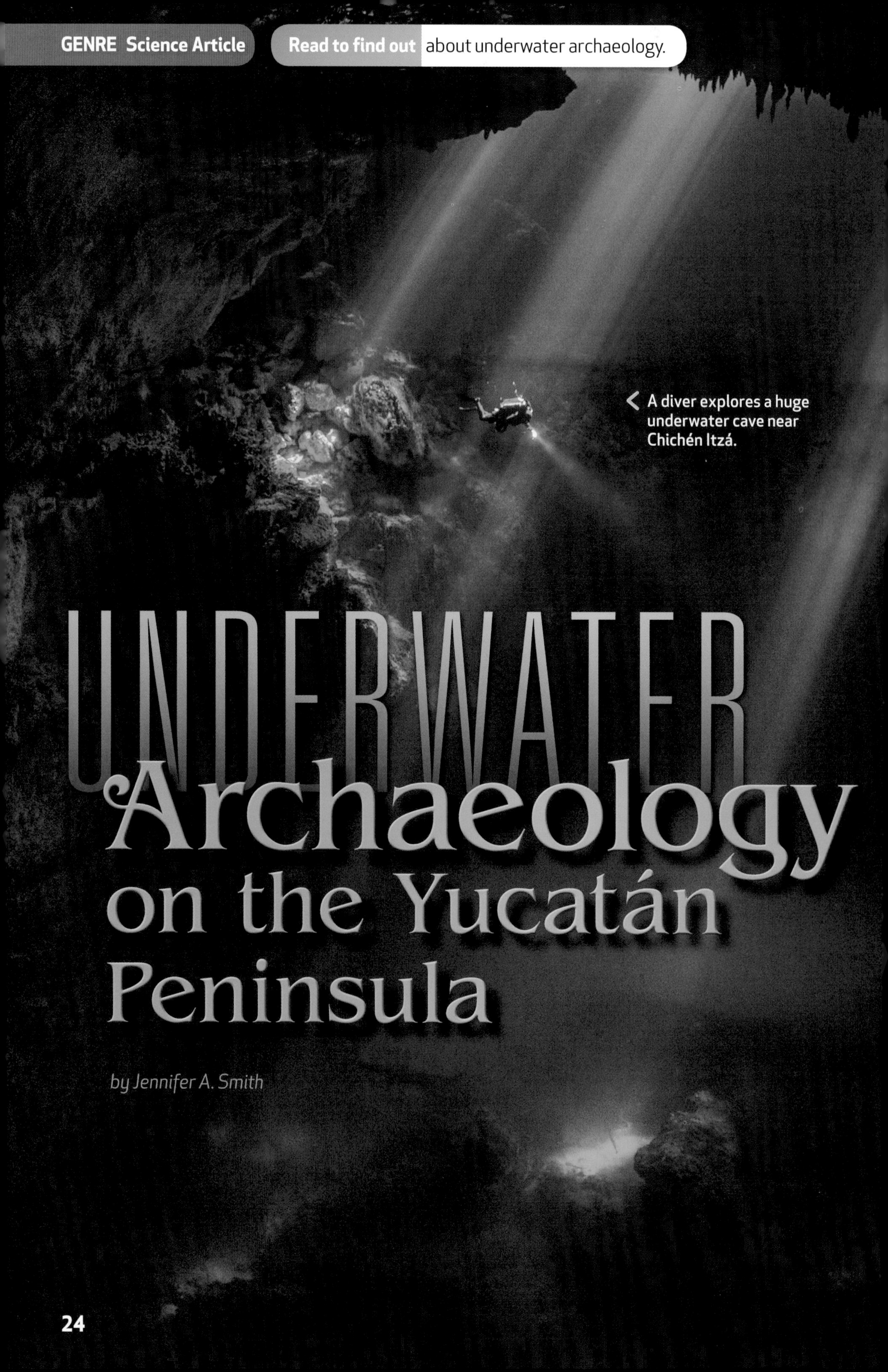

A diver explores a huge underwater cave near Chichén Itzá.

# UNDERWATER Archaeology on the Yucatán Peninsula

*by Jennifer A. Smith*

An archaeologist finds a cow skull at the bottom of an underwater cave.

What do you picture when you think of archaeologists digging up ruins of past cultures? Maybe you think of shovels, dirt, and dusty artifacts. But how about wet suits, air tanks, and flippers? Those are some of the tools of **underwater archaeologists**, who dive deep into the water to find objects that no one has seen or held for centuries.

Underwater archaeologists excavate and study artifacts they find on dives. To do their work, they must have training in archaeology and in diving, too. They work all over the world locating important objects in oceans, lakes, deep rivers, and underground water sources.

Underwater archaeologists face many challenges and dangers. Conditions underwater can be risky even for the most experienced divers, and diving to archaeological sites can be still more challenging. Divers deal with poor visibility in dark and murky water, which makes locating artifacts difficult. They can only be underwater for a short amount of time because the supply of air they carry with them is limited. The constant movement of water can bury artifacts under sand. And don't forget the normal hazards of diving—sharks, storms, seasickness. An underwater archaeologist might even come face-to-face with a crocodile on a normal day's work.

Read on to learn how underwater archaeologists on the Yucatán Peninsula have uncovered many clues to the daily lives, art, and religion of the Maya.

NATIONAL GEOGRAPHIC | EXPLORER

**GUILLERMO DE ANDA** Before becoming an archaeologist, Guillermo de Anda ran a successful dive shop. Diving in underwater caves is what first drew him into the world of underwater archaeology. Eventually, he closed his shop to study at a university in Mexico. De Anda is now a professor of underwater archaeology.

# DIVING Deep

National Geographic Explorer Guillermo de Anda is an underwater archaeologist. He and his team of students explore the Yucatán Peninsula's many **cenotes** (sih-NOH-teez), or huge, water-filled holes in the ground. Cenotes are made when acid from rain slowly eats through underground rock and carves out a cave. Over time, the cave grows very large, fills with water, and eventually collapses.

De Anda and his team dive into cenotes looking for signs of the Maya. They have found underwater temples during their dives. How did the Maya build temples underwater? According to de Anda, they didn't. The temples were built in the cenotes during terrible droughts when water levels were very low.

It may seem strange to build temples underground, but it made perfect sense to the Maya. They believed their gods lived beneath the ground in a mysterious underworld. The Maya built temples in the dry cenotes where they left gifts to please their rain gods. The Maya believed that if they pleased their gods, the gods would make it rain once again, ending the drought and filling the cenote with water.

As he is safely lowered into the water, de Anda checks out a cenote. The walls are covered with tree roots. Interesting rock formations hang from the ceiling.

# CHALLENGES Below

Descending into cenotes isn't easy work for de Anda and his team. The steep drop from the opening of a cenote to the water's surface can be hundreds of feet. The archaeologists need to carry cameras and scuba gear down into the cenote, which is also difficult. But descending isn't the only challenge. Bees and wasps often gather in cenotes. The team must bring a smoker along to fend off the stinging pests. Bees and wasps do not like smoke.

Looters pose another challenge to the archaeologists. Often these thieves have raided and disturbed a site before the team has been able to explore it. The team can only hope that's not the case before they start a dive.

Though underwater archaeologists face great challenges, they earn great rewards as well. In addition to temples, de Anda's team has found pieces of 1,000-year-old pottery, deer antlers, and even human remains in the cenotes of the Yucatán Peninsula. The artifacts and remains are sometimes tucked into ledges in the wall of a cenote. Without the hard work of de Anda and other underwater archaeologists, we would know far less about the Maya.

Archaeologists are sometimes lucky enough to find unbroken vessels. This vessel was found in a cenote on the Yucatán Peninsula. It is a container for holding food and water.

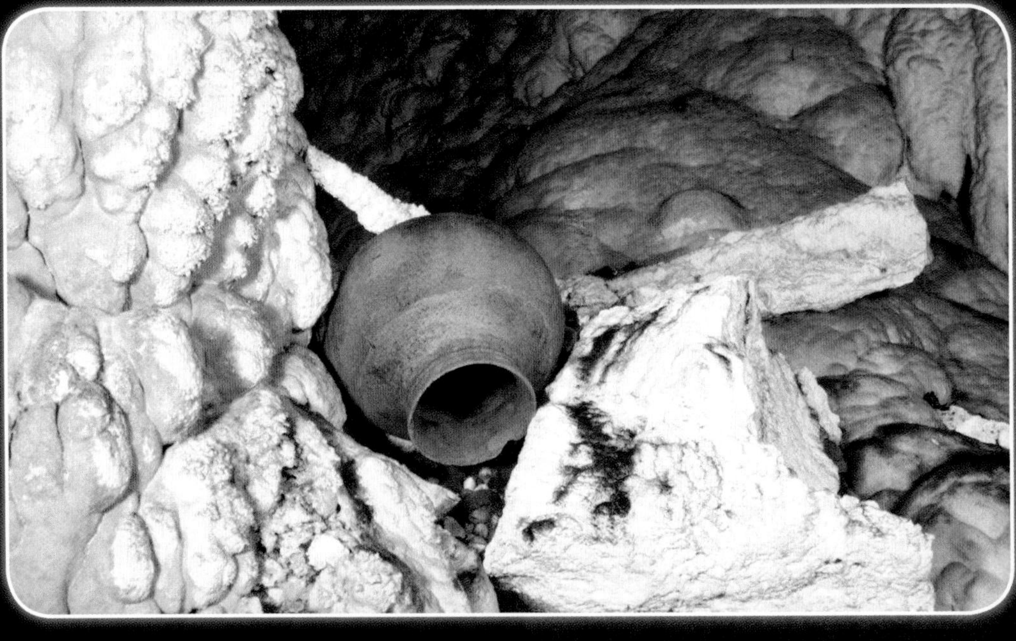

Guillermo de Anda shines a bright light on animal bones. He is diving in a cenote on the Yucatán Peninsula.

**Check In** What challenges do underwater archaeologists such as de Anda face when they explore cenotes?

GENRE Photo Essay   **Read to find out** about Maya artifacts.

# Maya Artifacts

*by Jennifer A. Smith*

**Archaeologists have discovered a great variety of artifacts the Maya left behind. From mysterious symbols carved in stone to beautiful examples of pottery, these artifacts give researchers clues about the lives of the Maya. What can these treasures from the past tell us?**

Archaeologists discovered this mask in Palenque, Mexico. It is made of a green stone called jade. Maya leaders wore jade masks during ritual ceremonies.

Around 250 B.C., the Maya developed a writing system based on **glyphs**, or pictures and symbols that represent letters and words. They drew glyphs on paper and painted them in murals that told stories of their history and the lives of their kings. They also carved glyphs into stone, like the ones shown here.

Glyphs give readers information without using words. Modern examples of glyphs can be found on street signs, computer screens, and even in this book.

Archaeologists found this colorful mural at an archaeological site in southern Mexico. Murals provide clues about how the Maya dressed, fought in wars, and thought about the world.

This **ceramic** sculpture is of a Maya leader sitting proudly on a throne. Archaeologists study the poses and clothes of the people carved into statues to learn about the Maya. In addition to creating images of important people, Maya artists made household items. Artists crafted plates, drinking cups, and bowls used for religious ceremonies.

**Check In** What do archaeologists learn about the Maya by studying murals?

## Discuss

1. What do you think connects the five selections you read in this book? What makes you think that?
2. How do ancient Egyptian pyramids and Maya pyramids differ? How are they the same?
3. What are some of the ways the Maya used chocolate?
4. How does underwater archaeology help us understand the Maya? Give at least two examples to support your answer.
5. What do you still wonder about the Maya? What would you like to learn more about?